Fun e
Rob
ch.

MW01602146

Praise for *Get Your Act Together*

"I wish I had a book like this when I was starting out my career. Gregg tells it like it really is on the long journey as a professional actor. Heed his words of advice and experience, it just may help you on your journey."

—Bryan Cranston
Emmy Award winning Actor, Director, Producer

"If you're an actor who wants to know how to get hired over and over again, please do yourself a favor and listen to everything Gregg Binkley has to say. No one is more prepared, professional and an absolute joy to work with. Making TV shows is hard and when you find people to surround yourself with who make it easier you've hit the jackpot. Gregg not only make the process easier, but he makes everything better by taking what you give him and making it his own. This book will show you how to do the same."

—Greg Garcia
Emmy Award winning Writer, Director, Showrunner

"I met Gregg years and years and years and years and years ago. We were both just two young handsome actors from Kansas trying to make a name for ourselves and trying to not be pigeon-holed by Hollywood casting directors for just our leading man looks.

This book is a great asset for aspiring actors and is full of so much helpful information and so many seasoned gems. From here on out, when someone asks me for career advice, I'll just hand them this book and say, 'Now scram kid!'"

—Eric Stonestreet
Emmy Award winning Actor

"I just finished reading Gregg's book. I know, you're thinking "not another 'how to act' book. Yes, but no. This little gem is concise, eminently practical, and filled with personal anecdotes that are entertaining and right to the point. The words come from a pro, an actor I've had the great pleasure of directing many times, one who was always prepared but was always ready to play and change. A director's dream. Read GET YOUR ACT TOGETHER and be a director's dream."

—Lee Shallat Chemel
Award winning Director and Producer
(Gilmore Girls, The Middle)

"I'd been a fan of Gregg Binkley's work as an actor on "Raising Hope," but not until he joined us for an episode I wrote did I become a fan of Gregg the person. He's smart, kind, humble, and a master of his craft. Armed with a deep tool box of choices, he infused the seriocomic role of a lovesick stalker (creepy but not dangerous) with so much humanity, our viewers were almost rooting for him. Plus, he's such a pro and a pleasure on the set, I can't wait to work with him again. Any actor starting out in this business should consider GET YOUR ACT TOGETHER a must read. Gregg's got chops for days, and he's put every ounce of his knowledge in these pages."

—Scott Williams
Writer-Executive Producer "NCIS"

I can think of few people better to help actors navigate the industry than Gregg Binkley. There is constant change in our business, and to have a career spanning decades is a remarkable feat. Read the book. Pay attention. Keep working."

—Garret Dillahunt
SAG Award winning Actor

"GET YOUR ACT TOGETHER is a practical and invaluable guide for the working actor. Filled with stories and wisdom from a 30 year career, Gregg guides you with great compassion through both the challenges and the well-earned victories that accompany a dedication to the craft. And that's what it takes, he reminds you — dedication: showing up for yourself and the work time and again until you're so good you can write a book about it."

—Jason Ensler
Director, Executive Producer

"Gregg made a name for himself by bringing his brilliant, versatile talent and genuine, approachable demeanor to every role. Casting directors love Gregg for his professionalism, clever humor, and consistent work ethic. Though I first discovered Gregg from the 2005 show "My Name Is Earl," he had been putting in the hard work many years prior. Actors will gain so much from his wealth of knowledge and decades of experience as an actor we all want to work with. Read this book and learn from a real pro. You'll be better for it."

—Jason Kennedy
Casting Director (NCIS)

As an acting coach and teacher, Gregg Binkley is patient, probing, intelligent, and his vulnerability and authenticity keep you honest in turn. He helps you break things down into doable actions to take power over your craft and career. When one studies with him/reads this book, one gains boots-on-the-ground-wisdom and experience from an actor's actor, with scads of knowledge and perspective about navigating this industry during all of its tumultuous seasons.

—Zehra Fazal
Actress, Award-winning voice artist

Gregg is as passionate about helping other actors expand their dreams as he is about building his own. A truly remarkable teacher and mentor"

—Maddison Bullock
Actress, Writer, Producer

"I have known Gregg Binkley for years. He has always been a wonderful person and a hilarious comedic actor. Now he is one of the best coaches and teachers I have worked with. Gregg helped me on so many auditions this past year and got me several bookings, but I am most grateful for him as the official acting coach for my directorial debut. His work is all over my film. Enjoy this book, enjoy Gregg, and enjoy your journey into acting and quite frankly, life. Gregg covers it all."

—Sean Whalen
Actor, Writer and Director

"To all of you who wonder: "How can I pursue a career in Hollywood and still retain those core qualities that make me proud of who I am and where I came from?" Look no further than Gregg Binkley! I have had the great pleasure of working with Gregg on two shows, and I am here to proclaim that this funny, hard working, talented, and kind man knows how to succeed in Hollywood and still be a great dad, friend, colleague, dude. Hollywood needs more Gregg Binkley. So drink in what he has to say, and then get out here and do as Gregg did and still does."

—Mike O'Malley
Award winning Actor, Writer, Showrunner

GET YOUR ACT TOGETHER

GREGG BINKLEY

Hardcover ISBN: 979-8-9894369-2-7
Paperback ISBN 979-8-9894369-0-3
eBook ISBN 979-8-9894369-1-0

Cover and interior design: thebookdesigners.com

Author photo: Brad Buckman Photography

Elevation Lane Productions
Los Angeles, California
www.elevationlaneproductions.com

For my wonderful wife Tokiko

"There is just one life for each of us.
Our own."

EURIPIDES 480-406 BC
Greek playwright

CONTENTS

A Midwestern boy on his own (1987)

INTRODUCTION

"If you believe it will work out, you will see opportunities. If you believe it won't work out, you will see obstacles."

WAYNE DYER

A career as a professional actor is one of the most enjoyable ways to make a living, but it is also one of the most challenging. I speak from experience. As of this writing, I have made my living as an actor for over 30 years and I have enjoyed some wonderful highs: A series regular role on a national network show for four years. A commercial spokesman for a restaurant chain for six years. Lead roles in two movies and supporting film roles with legendary directors such as Mel Brooks, Clint Eastwood, Woody Allen and the Coen Brothers. I have had recurring roles on 12 television shows and have continued to study and grow in my craft for these three decades.

I have also felt the extreme lows of this unpredictable profession: When will I ever work again? How does anyone ever get cast when the odds are so long every single time? How can I expect to provide for my family in Los Angeles when 90% of union actors don't even make $27,000 a year? How can I keep working as I get older when the industry is so focused on youthful, beautiful actors? How is it even possible? Why is it so difficult? When will it get easier?

As I have looked back at the successes of my career and looked forward to making it happen again, I have done some real soul-searching and extensive research. I want to share what I have learned with you. In the coming chapters I will give personal stories of my own journey, and lessons I have learned along the way. One of the main things I have realized is that I need to find a way to see clearly in a career that is so cloudy. If I can create for myself a daily approach to my work and my career, then I can give myself the best chance to attract what I want. You can do the same.

So much of this business is out of our control. Others are making decisions that will affect if / when/ where we will work. It seems chaotic because it *is* chaotic. We must accept that we can't control it. We can, however, affect it by the way we prepare and the way we present ourselves when our opportunities arrive.

My solution to it all is simple, but not easy. I will show you what I mean in the pages ahead, but what it ultimately comes down to is a focus on what we *can* control. What we can control is **our work ethic and our**

vision for our future. Those two things are what we own and no one can take those from us!

I wish I could give you five clear-cut steps for certain success as an actor. I can't. I can give you some clear steps for failure: Don't work on your craft. Spend your time complaining about how tough the business is. When you do get an audition, do half-hearted work because (your thought is) it's all about a "look" anyway. Sit around hoping, moping and coping.

The point of this book is to help you create a plan for your craft and your career, and to get you taking action in both areas. Ultimately, this is a book on how to *be* - in your acting scenes as well as in your *life*. These lessons are largely focused on the profession of acting but can definitely be connected to other professions as well. I want to share a healthy approach to the craft so you can go deep in your work, but also have a happy and rewarding life.

I encourage you to be on top of your game with your craft by constantly challenging yourself to explore your scenes in the moment, and allowing things to happen as they will based on what you (the character) want and the actions you take. You should also be constantly pursuing work by reaching out to new and old contacts, and making sure your team (agents, managers, etc.) is excited to work with you. Each chapter is an inspiration to raise your standards and trust in your own greatness. Be open to possibilities!

When we work as actors we often face two challenges in an audition room or on the set. **We have to be in command of ourselves, and we have to be in command of the character.** The first half of this book is largely devoted to getting command of yourself, and the second half is more focused toward command of the craft. We are on a journey with no guarantees financially, but so many rewards for our spirit. Acting is a calling, and I want to see you thrive.

But how can we work as actors by ourselves? How can we create for ourselves? How can we have a positive vision for our career when there are so many obstacles at every turn? Let's find our way. In my class, the "Working Actors Workshop," I tell my students during the first class that "this is a workshop I have created, but you should not think of it as *my* workshop - it is *your* workshop". I say the same to you about this book. It is a book I have written, but it is also *yours*. As you read the pages ahead, I will give you suggestions for your work ethic and your vision for the future, but I also encourage you to create your own plans. As the saying goes, "This is *my* way. What is *your* way? *The* way doesn't exist."

The acting profession will throw a lot of curve balls your way, but you have to keep swinging. I've always said, "I only take it personally *when* they hire me." My focus is on building a career. Every time I get an opportunity to audition for a role I want to do the best work I can, and I want to enjoy the experience with no attachment to the result. When I don't get hired for a specific role it could be for a hundred reasons, all of which have nothing to do with me. They decided to go with someone of a different weight or height or ethnicity or representative or gender or hairline or hair color or... or... or...

When you keep enduring the experience of not getting hired, it's easy to get disappointed or even worse, discouraged. It's important, though, to recognize that your mindset will determine how you prepare and how you will live in your work. When things are not going your way and you keeping getting knocked down, you can either give up or get up. Let me help you get up. You have a lot to offer.

I like the line from Hamlet, "The play's the thing." I'm taking the words out of context, but I like the idea of **play** being the key thing in our work and in our life. To be successful we have to do the work, but we should also have fun. I start every class with, "Let's get to work. Let's play."

Some people are interested in being a working actor. Some people are **committed** to being a working actor. If you're committed, let's get to work. Let's play.

It all started with Snoopy

CHAPTER ONE

BE OPEN

"Your present circumstances don't determine where you will go - they just determine where you will start."

LES BROWN

How do you begin your work on an acting scene? You start with the question, Who am I? When you are looking at a scene you must first determine who you are as the character, and your answer should not define you as separate from the character. You don't ask, "Who is he?" or "Who is she?" When becoming the character, you ask "Who am I?" The character is inside of you. As the great Meryl Streep puts it: "Don't spend any time looking at how you are different from the character. Find it all inside of you."

The same is true for your career: "Who am I?" Who are you in the business? What do you bring that no one else can? We will cover this more in Chapter Four, but the point is to find the keys for your character and your career within yourself. We are not all equal in the marketplace, but as we build a reputation with our unique talents, we can become actors who are in demand.

I invite you to open your mind to possibilities. Open your body to the freedom to play. Actors used to be called "Players" and I want you to start this book with the mindset of a person at play. There is a lightness, a joy, a feeling of anticipation and excitement that will serve you well when you think of it all as *play*. Open your heart to how you can serve through your work. If you are here to give, you will find your way to work.

Anyone can see roadblocks in this profession. Roadblocks will always be there, but so will openings and opportunities if you look for them. Be clear on what you want, and then jump into the unknown to get it.

I remember when I was a senior at the University of Kansas and I was trying to decide what to do for my career. I was about to graduate with a degree in journalism, but I didn't have a strong desire to go into advertising or broadcasting. As I contemplated my future, I decided to get quiet and open myself to possibilities.

I remember watching a show called *Inside the Actors Studio* where the host would interview successful actors and directors, and he would always end every episode by asking his guest, "If Heaven exists, what would you like to hear God say when you arrive at the pearly gates?" During the many seasons of the show the guests had a lot of interesting answers to that question, but the answer that always stuck with me came from Steven Spielberg. He said he would like to hear God say, "Thanks for listening."

So as I contemplated my future from my dorm room, I got quiet. I laid down on my bed and said, "what should I do?" and then I waited for a response. I listened. I was about to finish college and I could go anywhere or do anything. I had options. Of course I would have to start at the bottom of any company or business I chose, but for the moment I was able to choose my direction. "What should I do?"

As I considered what I thought were my possibilities, I would say them out loud. "Should I go into advertising?" I would wait and listen. "Should I go into broadcasting?" I would wait and listen. "Should I go into some other business? What should I do?" As I got quiet, the thought "Be an actor" kept coming to me. "Be an actor."

I hadn't really considered going into acting professionally because I had already decided I was "retiring" from acting after my last performance in high school. I swore off acting because I didn't love it anymore.

Here's what happened: The first time I ever acted was when I was in eighth grade. The theater teacher was going to be directing the play, *You're a Good Man Charlie Brown* and he needed someone to play Snoopy. He had seen me acting silly in the hallways and thought maybe I could be entertaining onstage too. I decided to give it a try, and although I was really not happy with the baggy dog costume I had to wear, I got onstage for the two performances and sang and danced and said my funny lines - and the audience loved it. I wasn't sure what to make of the response, but I just kept having fun. After all, it is called a *play*. I was playing!

After that great experience, I decided to participate in whatever shows the school was staging, and I also competed in the school's speech and drama competitions against other schools - an activity called Forensics. I won a lot of those competitions and just kept having fun.

As time went on, our teacher decided to bring in a local psychologist to teach us how to handle the pressure of performing in front of an audience. Many people get anxious onstage and the psychologist was brought in to teach us how to not be nervous. I had not had a problem with nerves, but I always wanted to learn so I followed his lesson. He said that when we get nervous, there is a place in our stomach that releases some liquid or something that goes into our system that causes us to feel nervous, and if we can control that liquid through his mental approach we won't be nervous. I don't know if I'm remembering the lesson exactly, but what I do know is he taught me how to be nervous! Suddenly I was getting nervous before every performance! I started to feel some liquid something in my stomach every time I performed! It got to where I was even throwing up before performances in high school. I wasn't *playing* anymore,

★

Be clear on what you want, and then jump into the unknown to get it.

♟

I was surviving a stressful activity. I decided to retire from acting at the ripe old age of 18.

But as I was finishing college, and I got quiet and asked myself what I should do with my life, "be an actor" kept coming to my mind. I'm not sure why I so easily followed my inner guidance, but I did. There is a line from the musical *The Man of La Mancha* that goes, "I'm Don Quixote, the Lord of La Mancha, my destiny calls and I go!" That is what it felt like for me at the time. Moving to Los Angeles "is my destiny, so I go!"

I remember two nights before I loaded up the car to move to Los Angeles, and I was at the dinner table with my Mom and Dad. They had been supportive of my move and seemed fine with my plans, but at dinner that night my dad said to me, "Well, how the hell are you going to make a living out there?" I was surprised by the question, but I remember my answer: "I'm not sure how, but I will."

I'm not sure how, but I will.

That is the mindset I encourage for all actors. We don't know exactly how we will succeed, but we know we will. The future happens not in the area of the known, but in the area of the unknown. Uncertainty. I faced the same challenge as I wrote this book. How can I help others when I don't know everything there is to know about the history of acting and every acting approach ever created? It's easy to become frozen into inactivity when you fear the unknown, but I realized that writing a book can be approached the same way as performing a scene. In our acting scenes, we determine what our character wants, and then we jump in. We must go for it and trust. That is where the magic happens, and that is where we have to rely on our gift as actors - our instincts. Each time I sat down to write, I reminded myself of where I was in the book, what I wanted - and then I trusted that the words and thoughts would arrive. I was surprised by how the right words would come to me at just the right time. This is the same approach we can take in our daily life as we move toward who we want to be.

So as we begin our journey here, I encourage you to be *open*. Be open to the possibilities of who you can be. Nelson Mandela said, "Who are you not to be magnificent?" You can't be magnificent by holding on tightly. You have to open up. Let go.

It's so easy to just say "it's impossible." That requires no thought, no effort. But I suggest you move your focus to a more productive and fun place: *Possibilities.* You are an actor, so take a moment to act and be creative toward how you can be a successful actor. I learned this lesson from Robert Schuller: Write down the numbers 1 through 10 and say to yourself, "If it was possible to get work - what would ten possibilities be?" Then write them down. Don't measure - just write. Make your list with ideas such as 1. Work daily on my craft. 2. Network constantly. 3. Visualize myself as a successful actor. Continue creating your list until you have at least ten.

In my classes, we always begin our new groups with this exercise and we usually come up with at least fifteen. When you approach the list with the mindset of it being a game, you can come up with creative ideas that suddenly make the impossible seem possible. As actors our job is to play, so as you approach your list and the other exercises in this book, be sure to work from ease.

It is easy to get intimidated by the challenges we face as actors, and if we are not careful we can let that fear keep us from taking action. A good way to overcome those fears is to embrace the approach of taking small steps.

What is one thing you can do for your craft today? What is one thing you can do for your career today? Start small. Start so small that you can't come up with an excuse. For your career you can say out loud, "I am a professional actor." That's easy. You can do that today. What else can you do? You can comment on a social media post from a casting director or producer that will remind them you are around. You can read an article in a trade magazine to see what's going on in the industry. Come up with something simple that you can do. What can you do for your craft today? You can do a one-minute vocal warmup. You can do something to open yourself up physically. Actors who are closed emotionally or who are physically inhibited cannot be dynamic artists. You can open yourself up physically by moving to music. You can work on one of your monologues. Find something simple to do. No pressure. It should be fun. Always start with the question, "What's one thing...?" Without the fear of the big question, your brain gets excited to find answers because it is not blocked by fear. You can always find something simple to do to get you started.

I encourage you to discover how taking small steps and creating new habits can change everything for you. In my classes, we add one new element each week and that helps make the growth completely manageable and not intimidating. When we approach our work this way, we allow for the compound effect. Over time you can create incredible results. You allow for Newton's Law of Physics - "An object in motion remains in motion unless acted upon by another force." As you move forward day by day, you create a growth momentum that can't be stopped. Eventually you will want to do more and more work, but the momentum happens by starting small.

I have always loved to share the renowned story of the Chinese bamboo tree. The Chinese bamboo tree begins as a tiny seed that a farmer plants in the ground. The farmer then fertilizes and waters the soil consistently for a year. Despite his efforts, there is no sign of growth after a year.

For a second year he consistently fertilizes and waters it again, but still there is no visible growth. He continues to nurture the seedling for a third year, and still there is no sign of change or growth. The farmer continues this diligent work even though it appears to be hopeless.

★

Be open to the possibilities of who you can be.

♕

For a fourth year, he continues to nurture the soil with water and fertilizer with the determination that he will one day have a bamboo tree. But after four years, still nothing has emerged from the soil.

Finally, in year five, the miracle unfolds. The Chinese bamboo tree grows 80-90 feet in just six weeks. So the question is: did it grow 90 feet in six weeks or did it grow 90 feet in five years?

The Chinese bamboo tree has a massive root system. Below the ground and out of sight, the work was happening to build the foundation for rapid growth. When the time was right, the bamboo tree was ready to become what it had prepared to be. In the acting profession, some actors appear to be an overnight success, but those actors would tell you their success came over time, not overnight. It takes commitment. As basketball legend Kobe Bryant said, "You have to work hard in the dark to shine in the light."

The Chinese bamboo tree would not have survived and thrived if the farmer had stopped faithfully watering the seed. Your dreams are the same. If you keep making sure the roots of your craft are growing and you have a strong vision for your career and you consistently take action, you may be surprised when (like the Chinese bamboo tree) it suddenly takes off when the time is right.

This kind of explosion of career growth has happened for me multiple times. I kept working on my craft and I kept working on my career and I was ready when the time was right.

Your pursuit of a long and successful acting career will take many turns, but when you are open to possibilities you will see many more options than the actors who focus on obstacles. You can consistently grow in your craft, but you can also create your own work; shoot your own scenes and write your own scripts. It's all available for you when you see possibilities. When we work on a film set, nothing happens that can be used until the director calls, "Action!" As we move forward, I encourage you to see yourself as the director and the lead actor in your life. Every action you take is a vote for the kind of person you want to be. Call action and *take* action!

★ Write down the numbers one through ten and ask yourself, "What are ten possibilities to book more work?" Then write them down. Don't measure, just write. Put your list of Ten Action Steps on your wall where you can see it every day. If you are interested in creating your own work, write down ten possible script ideas or characters you can create for an online production, television show or feature film. Open up your mind and write down at least ten.

★ Go outside and explore your environment. What do you see that you didn't notice before? Search for a specific color and see if you can find it. Get used to exploring in your daily life; this will serve you well in your work.

★ Try something new every day. It can be anything big or small. The habit of trying new things will get you ready for the unexpected. You won't be afraid of new challenges on the set if you are trying something new every day.

Dracula Dead and Loving It with the legend, Mel Brooks (1995)

CHAPTER TWO

BE A VICTIM NO MORE

You won't start winning until you stop whining.

As actors, our job is to take action in support of our character's wants, and to deal with obstacles as they come our
way. That pursuit is what makes the scenes interesting
to play and interesting to watch. When it comes to our
career, the obstacles we face may not seem very "interesting" but we can't move forward if they make us shrink.
We can either be intimidated or we can be motivated.

"Looks like you have a case of the PLOMs." I used
to hear that phrase as a kid. "PLOM" stands for "Poor
little old me." As we venture into a journey toward success as an actor, one aspect we have to free ourselves
from is victimhood: acting like a victim.

I studied for a while with acclaimed acting coach
Larry Moss, and I often think of his statement to our
class: "The bad news is, no one is going to save you. The
good news is, no one is going to save you." He was saying, you have to take care of yourself. You have to take

responsibility for your situation. This is a tough profession and we can't navigate the waters successfully if we get stuck complaining and feeling sorry for ourselves. You need to surround yourself with strong-minded people, and free yourself from those who spend their days complaining.

Everybody goes through tough periods and sometimes we need to explore why we may be struggling, but if we just focus on the struggle we will only get more struggle. If we focus on solutions, we will give ourselves the best chance to find new ways to grow and to book more work.

When we audition, it is imperative that we be in command of ourselves. We want to book the role, but *getting the job* is not where our focus should be when we audition. The audition *is* the job, so our focus should be on what is happening in the scene. If we place our focus on pleasing the people we are reading for - instead of on the work itself - that can lead to victim behavior.

All actors have horror stories about auditions, and my worst experience was when I read for a popular show called *Boston Legal*. My wife and I loved that show, and it was a dream of mine to work with the creator of the show, David E. Kelley. Not only is he a tremendous writer, but many of his shows were being shot in Manhattan Beach which is where I would love to live. When I received a great guest star audition for *Boston Legal* I was really excited.

I was going to read for the role of a young lawyer, and I quickly went to work on the sides. I knew I had a great chance to book the job because I had recently worked with the episode's director on a film, and he had requested me to read for the role. In my mind, I was definitely going to book this job!

As I prepared the sides, I made all the best choices for how I would play the scenes. Everything would be perfect. I would be doing scenes with William Shatner and James Spader; two actors I really admired. I knew the scenes would be great on my demo reel. I would also be bringing David E. Kelley's words to life, and I knew he would immediately like me and want to cast me as a regular on one of his other shows. I would then get to move to Manhattan Beach and have a beautiful house near the ocean and live happily ever after.

I arrived at the studios for my audition and thought of all things I would do to impress the producers. I kept going over my sides so I wouldn't make a mistake. Everything would be perfect. After I put my name on the sign-in sheet, I continued to work on the sides in the hallway as I awaited my turn. It all started to hit me - I had so much riding on this audition! I had to be perfect! If I could just book this job, it would lead to many more jobs and my house on the beach! I started to get really nervous. Really, really nervous. As I saw the other actors go in the casting room one after the other, I could feel my confidence disappearing. I realized I didn't know what I was doing. When they called me in the room, I didn't want to go - but I had to. My time had come.

As I entered the room I tried to get them to like me with a big friendly smile. I wanted them to know how much I wanted this role. I saw the director in there and I knew this was my big chance. The scene began and I needed to be perfect. After a couple of lines, I screwed up some words, and that caused me to be even more self-conscious. When I screwed up another line, I started to fumble with the papers to look for the line I had forgotten. I completely lost my place. I remember the executive producer saying, "It's okay Gregg, we like you. Start over." *They were feeling sorry for me*, I thought. *How pathetic!* I started again, I screwed up again. The rest of the experience is a blur, but I do remember it ended with me leaving the room drenched in sweat. I apologized, I made excuses, but the bottom line is I was not ready. I was not ready because I didn't know how to handle the situation.

In my workshop, I like to have one session where we explore how it feels to audition as a victim. When I was in high school we watched a video called *Scared Straight* where they showed prisoners talking about the horrors of life behind bars. The point of the video was to get the high school kids who were viewing the documentary to be so scared of prison that they would not commit crimes in the first place. I took that video as an inspiration to create a Victim Audition exercise. I wanted to show the actors

★

Sometimes we want something so much that we do too much.

♜

in my workshop how pathetic we look when we act like victims during industry meetings.

Before I describe the exercise, let's look at some common victim behaviors that actors do in auditions:

Apologizing

Asking unnecessary questions

Rushing through the scenes

Not listening

Giving excuses

Kissing up

Not leaving when the audition is over

In a casting session, the casting director, the director, and the producer are there to do a job. They are there to find an actor who matches what they are seeking for a specific role. They are not there to humor you, and they are especially not there to take care of you! Your job in the room is to play the character in a way that is truthful for you, and then allow it to happen in the moment. If they give you an adjustment, your job is to make the new direction truthful for you, and then allow it to happen in the moment. When the reading is over, you don't stay and try to make them like you with needy conversation. You say "thank you" and you leave. If you match what the producers want for the role, you will be cast. If someone else better matches up with what they are looking for, then that other actor will be cast. No amount of begging or kissing up will change that fact. However, if you act like a victim and they have to take care of you, it won't matter how well you do in the audition. They won't want to hire you for this role or any future roles. They won't want the headache.

For the Victim Audition, I have each actor come in the room and do these things: they enter with the mind-set "PLEASE LIKE ME!" Once they are in the room, they immediately apologize for something. Then they make an excuse for something. Then they ask for permission to do something. Then they ask an unnecessary question. When the audition starts, they rush through the scene. When it's over, they make an excuse for why it didn't go well. When they are offered direction for a second take, they do their second take exactly like the first one, because they didn't listen to the directions. When the second take is over, they don't leave. Instead, they make small talk and apologize for something and then ask more unnecessary questions or make unnec-essary statements about the role or the business. After the casting director has said, "Thanks for coming in" at least three times, they finally leave. Once the actors in class have experienced what it's like to behave that way in an audition, and after they see the other students act that way, they never want to behave that way again!

Sometimes we want something so much that we do too much. That feeling of desperation can lead you to embarrassing behavior. Everyone knows what it's like to spend time with needy people. When someone is desperate and clingy, you just want them to leave. Casting directors feel the same way about desperate actors. When you walk in a room, what energy do you bring? Are you an energy giver or an energy taker? Be the kind of person who elevates the energy in a room. You do that by being prepared and present and confident. As we move toward how to do that, let's let go of the victim mentality. It doesn't serve you well. You're better than that.

★ Catch yourself today when you are acting like a victim. Becoming conscious of your behavior is half the battle. If you are acting needy, just stop. Either say nothing or phrase your comment in such that you take responsibility for your situation.

★ See yourself as an equal. When you encounter anyone today, silently say to yourself, "I am equal to you" no matter if that person is considered to be in a higher or lower position than you. Make sure you see everyone as colleagues.

★ Be conscious of rushing to please someone today. If you notice you are rushing, take a breath and slow down. You will gain more command of yourself as you get in the habit of being mindful and slowing down.

Kenny James on *My Name is Earl* (2005-2009)

CHAPTER THREE

BE PRESENT

"Life is only available in the present moment."

THICH NHAT HANH

There is no better place to be than right here, right now. Here is where the magic is - both in life and in our acting scenes. Accessing the here and now is vital to being a great actor and a successful one. Now is all we have, so let's embrace it. Let's work from effortless ease.

I believe the main gift we have as actors is our instinct. How can we access our instinct? There are many ways, but it eventually comes down to stillness. The great actor Michael Caine said, "The work is the relaxation." How can we be relaxed when so much is supposedly on the line in an audition or on the set? Like everything else, it comes down to habits. Take some time each day to be present. Be right here, right now.

One way to get present is to ask yourself, "am I breathing?" Your answer to that one question will get you to the present moment because it will make you aware of your breathing, which is happening right now. If you're nervous, you will notice your breathing is probably fast, but at least you are noticing it. As you ask that question more often, you will be able to make adjustments. To calm yourself, practice this pattern of breathing: Breathe in to the count out six, hold for the count two, then breathe out slowly to the count of seven. That breathing pattern can slow your heart and get you to a place of awareness.

Another way to get present is to name colors. Look around you right now and slowly name the colors you see. Make sure you speak out loud the name of each color in a full sentence such as, "that shoe is brown." Truly see it and take a few seconds to keep looking at the object - get present with it then move on to something else. "That carpet is tan." Keep looking at that item until your complete focus is on that item, then move to another. "That door is white." Take a moment with each item and it will enable you to get present.

I will never forget when I auditioned for the pilot episode of the hit show, *My Name is Earl,* created by Greg Garcia. I was fully prepared, so all that was left for me to do before the audition was to get present. I waited outside the office at the studio and looked all around me. I named what I saw. "That tree is brown"... " those leaves are green"... "that car is red"... I continued for while. Then I reviewed my audition scene. The casting director still hadn't called me in to audition. Back to colors: "That roof is brown"... "that fire hydrant is yellow"... They finally called me in. As I walked down the hallway, I continued to notice colors. "That carpet is tan... that painting is blue..." When I got to the audition room, the people inside saw someone enter with presence. They saw an actor who looked confident because he clearly wasn't nervous.

The role I was auditioning for was a character named Kenny James. Earl had picked on Kenny when they were both younger, and now Kenny would be coming face to face with his tormentor in the scenes I would be playing. Kenny was also gay, and in one scene would confess that fact to Earl. I asked a friend how her brother revealed to her that he was gay. She said her brother cried when he told her. When the audition scene came to the point where Kenny was to tell Earl he was gay, I cried. At that very moment, the phone rang in the casting director's office and the audition was interrupted. At an earlier point in my career I would have let that interruption derail me, but this time it didn't bother me. I was present. The casting director answered the phone, and then Greg asked me to do the scene again without crying, and I did. I did the other scenes as well and then left. I had been completely present.

I make a point of sharing this story with you because I ended up booking the role of Kenny for the pilot. I went on to do 20 episodes during the four-year run of the show. Greg later created the hit show *Raising Hope* for Fox. He cast me as Barney Hughes on that show, and

I eventually became a series regular and was in 71 episodes. I don't believe those 91 episodes of network television would have happened had I not been fully alive in that one audition where I got myself completely present by naming colors.

Another way to get present is with meditation. Everyone has heard that meditation can clear the mind and get you centered, but most people still don't do it. There are many reasons for that, the biggest of which is your ego doesn't want you to meditate and it feeds you with excuses such as, "You don't have time." "It's not really necessary." "You'll do it tomorrow."

Making time for meditation can be a challenge, but when you recognize the benefits it will inspire you to find the time. Our lifetime is created one day at a time, and how we handle each day leads us to a life of stress or life of ease. I have learned that when I meditate regularly, I am able to handle potentially stressful situations with ease. I feel that way on the set because I feel that way every day. I don't have to hope to be present under pressure if I'm present all the time.

I benefited from Wayne Dyer's "ah" meditation which you can find online. In it, he guides the listener to meditate for 20 minutes using the sound of "ah" which he said is the sound of creation. I did that meditation regularly and was always sending out the intention that one day I would become a series regular on a national network show. Whether it was a vibrational result of the meditation or just the fact that I had consistently focused on what I clearly wanted, my dream eventually came true.

Everything we want to create comes from how we act in the here and now. Meditation will relax your body and mind so you can be open and free to what is happening in the moment. The key is to become relaxed and present so you can bring that awareness into your work. The great actor Bill Murray said it well: "Someone told me some secrets early on about living. You have to remind yourself that you can do the very best you can when you're very, very relaxed. No matter what it is, no matter what your job is, the more relaxed you are, the better you are."

When you watch Bill Murray's work, you will see almost no tension. He is always available in his work and he allows his impulses to take him wherever they will. That's the kind of brilliant work we all love to watch. The ability to allow in the moment - that is where the magic is. We cannot try to achieve a moment, we have to allow it. Acting is accessing. When you get yourself to a place of stillness, you will have access to your instincts.

There is only one place you can be at a given time in your life - right where you are. That is true in your acting as well. When you know your lines completely and you know your character's intentions, but you don't know exactly how the scenes will play out, you will find the true joy of acting. This approach will also lead to your best work because everything will be happening in the present moment.

If "allowing" is the most fun and leads to your best work, why don't we all do it? The reason is - we all want to control. We want to know in advance that everything will be okay and we will survive. We want to protect ourselves. But "safe" acting will not thrill you or the viewer. We might watch it and note that the actor has made some interesting choices, but we won't be moved toward anything but an observation of an actor acting.

I remember on the set of *Raising Hope* my friend Garret Dillahunt, who played Burt, told me I had great instincts and I should trust them more. I appreciated his words, but old habits die hard. I had been trained in the ways of planning out a scene. I would break down the scene and make specific choices of how I would feel at each given moment. I planned out every detail in advance and did my best to survive the scene and get to the finish line without messing up. I was afraid to make a mistake, so I was often anticipating the next moment. My performances may have come off as smart, but I usually wasn't truly present.

There are good reasons to do scene breakdowns. We need to know what is going on for our character and we need to know what is going on in the scene. But if we get locked into playing the scene exactly as we had planned it all out in advance, we will only be present to what is going on in our own head. When we do that, we don't

★

*When you
get yourself
to a place
of stillness,
you will have
access to your
instincts.*

have the excitement of the now - the present. It's like a boxer going in the ring with a plan for how he will execute each round. He will start with an upper cut, then a right cross, then a left hook... But what happens when his opponent throws an unexpected punch? He gets knocked on his ass. The same thing happens to us in an acting scene if we aren't ready to go with what is happening in the moment. When you simply try to execute your plan, you become a technician not an artist.

A good exercise to make sure you are present in your scenes is one I learned from acclaimed acting coach Howard Fine. It's called the Repeat Exercise. When doing your scenes in rehearsal, repeat the last sentence the other character says before you say your next line. The other actor repeats your last sentence before they say their next line. When you do this back and forth throughout the entire scene, you will recognize that you have to listen and respond. This exercise is good to do right before recording a self tape as well. It prepares you to be present and respond in the moment.

The ability to be fully present will lead to your best work. When the actor is at ease the audience will be too. As you commit to a daily practice of present moment awareness, you will discover that your work and your life will be more fulfilling. Life is happening right here, right now. When you bring that presence to your life, people will love spending time with you. When you bring that presence to your scenes, the audience will watch.

★ Ask yourself, "am I breathing?" That simple question will give you an awareness of your breathing and will bring you to the present moment.

★ Take at least one minute each day for meditation. You can find a variety of meditations of different lengths to practice online.

★ Name colors. Look around and name at least five colors you see. Really connect to each color as you name it, and then eventually move on to the next one. This practice helps you to focus on the here and now.

Malcolm in the Middle with Bryan Cranston (2003)

CHAPTER FOUR

BE UNIQUE

"You might as well be yourself.
Everyone else is already taken."

OSCAR WILDE

As I mentioned earlier in the book, after 30 years I had basically achieved all I wanted to as an actor. I played lead roles in films, I had been a commercial spokesman, and most importantly for me - I had been a series regular on a national network show and that show went into syndication. I reached my goal. I also had a wonderful family with my wife and three children. I had climbed the mountain.

What I didn't fully embrace at the time was I still had a long way to go... I couldn't continue to live off past accomplishments, I had to keep moving forward. My kids were young, I was still relatively young, and I eventually realized another mountain was in front of me. Maybe a bigger mountain than the one I had already climbed. I had spent a lot of time wishing *Raising Hope* would have lasted many more years so I could have coasted longer, but that wishing was getting me nowhere. Looking back now, I can see that I went through the five stages of grief: Denial. Anger. Bargaining. Depression. Acceptance.

Getting to acceptance was the key. If I didn't accept where I was, I would just continue to spin my wheels. I had to truly accept where I was and also accept that I still had a lot to offer!

The big change for me came when I went to a Foundation Class taught by Howard Fine. His nine-week course took me back to the basics of acting and also introduced me to the notion of using *myself* in my work. Up until that point, I usually created the characters I played by *acting* like them rather than *being* them. Over my career, I had become good at performing as though I was connected to what I was saying and doing as the character, but most of the time I was just acting. The words and actions weren't truly coming from me. Howard coached me to find authentic connection and investment. I learned that I should not try to *act* like the character, but instead find every character within me.

I have used these lessons in my own work and with my own classes, and it has helped me find the love for acting again. Over time, I also found my love for coaching and my love for public speaking because I realized I can find my message within me. I just have to tap into it. I have to be vulnerable, courageous, and intuitive - all essential attributes of a great actor.

What separates me and what separates you is our uniqueness. Our spirit. Our essence. As artists we are all unique. We have a desire to express ourselves through our art and that is where we find true joy. Unfortunately, once we start looking for work, we begin to think about "what they want." How can we please them? How can we give them what they are looking for? How must we play this scene to book the job?

There is value in recognizing what is needed by directors, producers and casting directors when it comes to the tone of a show or film, but when you go beyond that and try to please them with how you interpret a role, you lose your power as an actor. When you embrace a role by finding it within you and express your talent by bringing a character to life as you see the character, you gain your power and you find your joy.

Bryan Cranston has always been one of my favorite actors and I have a particular fondness for him because of the time he sought me out for a role. He was in the main cast of the hit show *Malcolm in the Middle,* and he occasionally was chosen to direct episodes. He was going to direct an episode where they were casting a character who was an uptight and demanding assistant night manager of an electronics store. At the time, I was in the middle of a six-year commercial campaign where I was the spokesman for Del Taco. The character I was playing in the commercials was innocent, enthusiastic and goofy - the opposite of the characteristics of the assistant night manager. I had never met Bryan before, but he had seen my commercials and he thought I could be good for the role.

I read for the producers and I booked the job. Later, when we were on the set I asked Bryan why he had requested me for a role so different from my Del Taco character. He said, "a good actor is a good actor." He trusted that I would find my own unique way to interpret the role, and he gave me a chance. When you look at Bryan Cranston's career you will see he has been constantly growing as an artist, but he always brings his uniqueness to his roles. No one can play the characters he plays the way he does. When you find the characters you play within you, no one can match what you do.

I love Harold Guskin's book, *How to Stop Acting*. In it, he shares how he worked with terrific actors such as Kevin Kline, Glenn Close and James Gandolfini. One of the unique approaches that Guskin would take with his actors is a technique he called "taking it off the page." At the beginning stage of working on a character, he would recommend taking the lines one by one and finding how you can make those lines real for you. Take a breath, read the line and then say it out loud in a way that is real for *you*. Find your own personal connection to each line as you explore them one by one. How can this line be real for *you*? You find your personal connection line by line, and as you do this exercise you begin to find the character within you. Ultimately you, of course, do your

★

When you find the characters you play within you, no one can match what you do.

⩒

research on the character, but all along the way you find your own personal connections. When you invest in the work and interpret the role in a way that is true for you, you will offer a unique approach that no one else can or will. As you continue to work this way, you will find your love for the craft. *Eventually you can be an actor who is sought out because you stand out.* It all begins by trusting that you have something to offer that no one else has. Christopher Nolan has said he casts "to an energy that is memorable." That energy cannot be forced, it comes from the authenticity of the actor.

Stephen Sondheim wrote many classic musicals and one lyric has particularly stood out to me. It is from the song "Move On" from *Sundays in the Park with George*: "Anything you do, let it come from you, then it will be new."

In your work, each character you play will be different from you, but you can still find each character within you. In your personal life your personality is based on how you think, how you act, and how you feel. Those elements have all been established over time. When you are playing a character in a production you need to discover how that character thinks, acts and feels. As you do your research and as you continually rehearse, you will find your way to justify why your character thinks as he does, why he acts as he does, and what causes him to feel as he does. You will be playing a new character while still using yourself. The character then won't be different from you. It will be you.

You can't blend in and stand out at the same time. When you find the truth of the character within you, your work will be unique and you will stand out. Your uniqueness is key. When the material comes through you, the acting goes away. Whether you use your imagination or connect to real sources or use a combination of both, you will ultimately be bringing yourself into the circumstances of the character.

Meryl Streep is known for the wide range of characters she has played throughout her career, but she has said that each character comes from within her. "Acting is not about being someone different," said Streep. "It's finding the similarity in what is apparently different - then finding myself in there. I don't visualize the person, I visualize aspects of me that I can enhance to be this person. So I don't see a different person than myself, but I see things about me I can shift or emphasize or de-emphasize to make this character." One of the all-time great character actors says she finds the characters she portrays not from the outside, but from the inside.

When you personalize the character you are playing, the words and actions will become true for you, and that will lead the audience to want to watch and listen. Consider how you react when listening to someone telling a personal story. You are engaged because the story lives inside the storyteller. You know it's true. The same thing applies to our acting work. If the words and actions of the character live within you, it will be true and the audience will watch and listen. It must not merely come *from* you, it must come *through* you.

I believe the same is true in your real life. When you look within to find the person you are meant to be, you will find your uniqueness. That uniqueness will make you stand out. All great people stand out because they have embraced who they truly are. Whether it's in your day to day life or in the lives of the characters you play, I encourage you to find it all within and then enjoy letting it out.

★ Before you go to sleep at night, write down the unique experiences you witnessed in your life and in the lives of others that day. This daily awareness will help you discover script ideas and character ideas you can use in the work you create. This practice will also help you appreciate the value of each day.

★ Take a scene from a script and explore it line by line to find your personal connections to each line. Be free. It's more important to be free than to try to be "right." Make each line true for you and you will find your connection to the character you are playing.

★ Trust yourself. Trust yourself. Trust yourself.

Revenge of the Nerds 3: The Next Generation (1992)

CHAPTER FIVE

BE CONFIDENT

"Attach your confidence to your intentions,
not your current ability."

WAYNE DYER

One of the key traits of successful people is self confidence. What's important for us to recognize is that those people found their confidence before, not after, their success.

Early in my career, I had my first opportunity to read for the lead role in a film. It was a made-for-television movie called *Revenge of the Nerds 3*. (It was a story that apparently needed to be told a third time). I remember before the final audition, the nerves that overcame me in high school started to return. I could feel my fears coming up and my focus shifting from what could go right to what could go wrong. I was in my one-bedroom apartment in Sherman Oaks and I had to face the reality of my situation. I was letting fear get the best of me.

Instead, I reminded myself that I deserved this opportunity. The director had requested me, and I understood the character I was playing. I knew I could do this! If I sensed someone in the audition room was not supporting me, I had to let that go and focus on my work instead. I remembered reading a quote from one of my favorite actors, Martin Short. He said, "you have to be your own best cheerleader." I stood outside the audition room and silently gave myself the best pep talk I could, and then I went in. I played the scenes in the moment and gave what I had to give. My confidence paid off and I got the role - my first lead role in a film.

In that film, my character, Harold Skolnick, was the leader of the new generation of nerds. One of the other characters was played by Grant Heslov who went on to become a very successful film producer. The other main characters were played by a number of comedians, and one of the those was Chi McBride. Chi had no experience but he had talent and most impor- tantly, he had confidence. It turns out that confidence took him to amazing places. Of all the actors I worked with on that film, Chi went the furthest in acting. He was a series regular on *Hawaii Five-O, Pushing Daisies, Boston Public,* and *The John Larroquette Show* as well as playing strong roles in many major motion pictures. I read an interview with him in *Backstage West,* and he said he owed it all to his practice of confidence.

I have noticed that many people with genuine talent

often question themselves and wonder if their work is any good. That kind of awareness helps them continue to find ways to grow, but if they aren't careful they can let their doubts keep people from seeing their talent. Imagine you are casting a show and your career as a producer depends on a successful run. The actors you cast will control the fate of your show with their performances. Will you choose the actors shaking with nerves and insecurities or the ones who work with command and confidence? The choice is obvious. We must be confident, but how?

The first step to confidence is to be fully prepared with your work, which we will cover in more detail in Chapter Six. It is also important to know where to place your attention once you get in the audition room or on the set. When we are nervous it is because we are placing our attention on ourselves, and that only feeds the nerves. You need to place your attention somewhere else, that is why the naming of colors exercise we did in Chapter Three is so valuable. When we do that exercise, we are sending our focus outward. There is more tension when we try to hide the nervousness, but when we focus our attention outward, the tension disappears. It's like an athlete playing a game. As soon as the game begins, the tension leaves. The key is to send your focus out early.

For example - when you walk into a room, look to see what the other people are wearing. See if they are wearing glasses, notice the colors of the walls, etc. When you practice this approach regularly, you will get used to sending your focus outward. Once the reading of the scene begins, place your focus on sending the message that you (as the character) are sending to the other character. See if your message is landing or not. Your focus is all outward. This approach keeps you from focusing on any insecurities you feel on the inside.

There are other steps we can take every day to build our confidence. One simple exercise is called a Confidence Space Walk. I learned this when I studied with acting coach Stephen Book, and in this exercise you fill your body with confidence either seated or preferably as you walk. You may think this exercise is silly, but open yourself up to experiencing it. If confidence isn't a habit of yours, this exploration can help you build confidence in your body.

Take your time as you go through this exercise. Begin with your toes as you walk or sit. Move your toes and feel your toes as if they are confident. Try not to judge. Move your toes with confidence. Now move your whole foot with confidence. Now your shins and calves. Let some time pass and then move on to your knees. Your thighs. Your pelvic area. Now your entire body from the legs down is filled with confidence. Move with confidence. Walk in that confidence.

Now move to your stomach and feel confidence there. Your lower back. Your chest. Take your time. Feel

★

When we focus our attention outward, the tension disappears.

confidence in the front of your shoulders. Your biceps and triceps. Feel confidence in your forearms. Your hands. Your fingers. The back of your shoulders. Now your whole body from the neck down is filled with confidence. Walk in that confidence.

Now feel confidence in your neck. Your chin. Your mouth. Your teeth. Your nose. Your eyes. Your ears. Your eyebrows. Your forehead. The top of your head. Your whole body is confident now. Feel the energy all around you. It's all confident. Walk in that confidence. Greet people with that confidence.

This Confidence Space Walk is something you can do anytime, anywhere. Walk this way as you walk through a grocery store or as you walk your dog around the neighborhood. Do this daily, and it becomes who you are. Decide to have a day where you will bring confidence to all your activities. As you remind yourself to do this, you will notice how often you *lack* confidence. Take a moment to fill your body with confidence, and then see how you behave differently. Notice how you speak differently. As you choose to bring confidence to your daily activities, it will slowly but surely become second nature.

One of the essential characteristics of all successful actors is courage. It takes courage to perform in front of strangers, and it definitely takes courage to choose to make your living as an actor. You must have trust in yourself. You can build that trust by the way you

approach each day. When you build the habit of prac-
ticing your craft and taking steps for your career each
day, each week, each month, you eventually recognize
that you deserve success. You're not entitled to it, you
deserve it. You have done the work and you are ready to
work. You know you have something valuable to offer.
That is confidence.

Anyone who has risen to the top in the entertain-
ment industry had confidence in themselves *before* they
became successful. Just because you may not be a working actor now doesn't mean you can't *see* yourself as a
working actor now.

If you listen to casting directors and producers,
you will hear them say that confidence is an essential
ingredient when they are casting. There are so many
quotes I could share with you here, but one I particularly like was from the great director and producer
Garry Marshall: "Some people just aren't ready," he
said. "They are still going through the 'I'm nervous
at an audition' stage. You haven't got time for that. No
shoot for television or movies is longer than five minutes. All we're asking for an actor is to *be secure for five
minutes.* We don't care if before they're throwing up
or after they're throwing up. I've been there. I know
those five minutes - that's the money."

Anytime we do our work in an audition room or on
a film set, we will encounter surprises. We will always
have to deal with something uncomfortable. The great

actors learn to be comfortable being uncomfortable. They turn to their confidence to navigate them through any situation.

When you practice your confidence daily, you will grow daily. When your opportunity comes, you won't have to try to manufacture confidence - it will be who you are. When you go to an audition, recognize that there's nothing to be afraid of. What's the worst that can happen? You don't get the job? You already don't have the job. The worst has already happened! The pressure is off - so go have fun. Your confidence compels people to work with you. Your neediness repels them. Move forward with confidence.

★ Practice a Confidence Space Walk at least once a day. Notice how intentionally walking with confidence changes your demeanor and the way you speak.

★ As you enter a room, think of yourself as the host rather than a guest and notice how that affects your behavior. Decide to give rather than to get. That is the mindset of someone who is confident.

★ Do something today with complete confidence: The way you interact with a clerk. The way you handle a phone call. The way you walk to work. See how it feels to find that confidence within you.

Del Taco Commercial Campaign (2000-2006)

CHAPTER SIX

BE PREPARED

*"Everyone has the will to win. The question is:
do you have the will to prepare to win?"*

BO EASON

Preparation gets you ready for opportunities and your time to shine. Many actors spend their time complaining about a lack of work, and then when they get an audition they aren't ready! The actor's focus has been in the wrong place. Had the casting director requested the actor recite a list of complaints about the acting profession, the actor would have been completely prepared. Unfortunately, the casting director was interested in the actor's work, not the actor's whines.

When you have a role to play, you have a responsibility to bring the character to life truthfully. You're not going to *act* like some other person, you are going to *be* this person as you interpret the character from within you. Let's cover some basic but essential areas of preparation as you build the character you are bringing

61

to life, and then let's see how this approach can apply to our own lives.

The first thing I like to do when I get some sides for an audition is to read it out loud at least 20 times. I don't just read my lines, I read everything. As I read it out loud, I make every effort to not make any decisions on how to play the scene. Many actors will read their lines once or twice, make decisions on how they will present those lines, and then they will rehearse those choices over and over to solidify the choices.

I prefer to read the entire scene out loud at least 20 times and let the scene begin to work on me. I will let the character work on me. I will read the scene different ways and explore what is happening. The more I do this approach with a free mind, the deeper my understanding becomes of the scene and the character. Then I can begin to answer these questions: Who am I? Where am I? What is my relationship with the other people in the scene? What do I want? What actions will I take to get what I want? If I get a script where I play a main character and there is a lot of information to draw upon, I will also answer the question: What is my overall objective?

Who am I? Don't put distance between you and the character. Don't ask, "Who is he?" or "Who is she?" The question to answer as you create the character is, "Who am I?" As soon as you get the character breakdown, begin referring to your character in the first person: "I am an architect who is a single dad with three kids" or "I am a prostitute living on the downtown streets of Philadelphia" or "I am a second grade teacher at a small private school in Beverly Hills" or "I am a corporate lawyer with an addiction to pain medication," etc. Who are you as this character? It's all within you. Do a full examination of the history of you as this character. Never judge your character. Completely justify who you are and what you do.

Where am I? Where does this scene takes place? Are you comfortable or uncomfortable at this location? Is it indoors and if so, what is surrounding you? Is it outdoors and if so, is it cold? Is it muggy? Are there bugs? Is there traffic noise in the distance? Explore it all. Bring it all to life truthfully for you, using all your senses.

What is my relationship with the people in the scene? Look at each person and determine where you are in your relationship with those people (and you need to see them as real people not characters). As you examine these relationships, consider what substitutions you can use for them. If you have a scene with a secretary who is judgmental, consider using someone in your life who you know to be judgmental. If your relationship with the other character is one with a lot of guilt, you can put yourself in the proper mindset by using someone who you personally feel guilty around. You can often use elements from your real life and play them out in the scenes you are doing. As actress Carrie Fisher put it, "take your broken heart and turn it into art." Completely examine your relationships with everyone in the scene and fill it all up with truth for you.

What do I want? Actors can use the word "want" or "objective" or "intention," but it all comes down to what you *want* from the other person in the scene. I encourage you to state your want in such a way that it requires a response from the other person. State your want with phrases such as: "To make you _____ " or "To get you to _____" For example: "To make you love me" or "To get you to feel sorry for me," etc. When you state your want or objective this way, you will stay active to see if the other person is responding or not. As you do the scene, you will be noticing throughout if your plan is working. Be sure to supply the WHY for your wants. Don't be self-indulgent. Send your message to the other character. It is important that you stay active as you pursue your wants.

What actions will I take to get what I want? The tactics you use in pursuit of your *want*, are your *actions*. If your scene has you trying to get a character to date you, what actions will you take? Will you humor her, flatter her, impress her? The script will give you the words to say, but what *actions* will you take with those words? If you are a boss and you want an employee to quit, what actions will you take? Will you intimidate him, comfort him, ignore him? Be clear with your tactics and make sure you understand what is at stake for you (the character) in the scene. Also be sure to supply the WHY for your tactics. There is a reason you take the approach you take, and you need the justify the WHY within you. <u>If you are fully engaged in your actions, the audience will be fully engaged in watching you.</u>

I have always liked this quote from the great actor, Alan Alda - "I think before any actor enters a scene, it should be necessary to pass under a sign that reads: 'You are not allowed on this stage unless you *want* something with all your heart and soul *and* you have a way of getting it.'"

What is your overall objective? As you examine the script, determine what your overall objective is as this person (character). If you have a complete film, television or play script and your character is one of the main characters, you will have a lot of material to examine. If your character is just in a couple of scenes you won't have as many clues to use, but it's still exciting to consider. You don't want to impose something that isn't appropriate, but you do want to be clear on how your character sees the world. A good way to phrase your answer is: My name is _____ and my world is _____.

One last question: What do you love about playing this character? So often we may think of our preparation as being hard work, but we should think of it as play. When you consider what you *love* about playing the character, your focus will be on the joy of acting. Find where the character lives inside of you and love the opportunity to bring the character to life in your own

★

Actors aren't hired for their potential, they are hired for what they can do right now.

♙

unique way. The more you know yourself, the more you will see yourself in every character.

When you have answered these questions, it's time to rehearse. Consider what mindset and state of emotion your character is in. For example, to get yourself in the proper state you can say aloud three times phrases such as: "Why did you betray me?" or "I'm so happy to see you!" or "I just don't trust you." Using and repeating some quick message that is associated with your character's circumstances can trigger you into the appropriate mental and emotional state.

You can also experiment with preparing your physical state by using the breathing patterns, body postures, and facial expressions for certain emotions. I remember seeing footage of legendary actor Jack Nicholson getting ready for the classic scene from *The Shining* where his character slams an axe through the bathroom door to get at his wife, Wendy. Before the cameras started rolling, he stalked around the room and emotionally talked out loud to make sure his body and mind were ready for what his character was about to do. He was breathing as his character would be breathing. There are standard breathing patterns for certain emotions that you can use to get your body ready for a scene. For more information on this approach you can seek out Alba Emoting instructors to get a full understanding of their techniques, but here are some notes for the breathing patterns for six basic emotions:

For Happiness: Have a relaxed body and a large open smile. Eye brows up and open. Breathe in through the mouth with one main inhalation and out through the mouth in rapid exhales. This is a great way to trigger laughter.

For Anger: Have a tensed body, lips tightly closed, tensed eye muscles and flared nostrils. Eyes half closed. Breathe with sharp breaths in and out of the nose.

For Fear: Have a tensed body inclined slightly backward with your eye brows lifted and your eyes wide open. Breathe using shallow breaths through a wide open mouth, almost gasping for air.

For Sadness: Have a relaxed body, and your eyes gazed downward. Breathe in through the nose and then out through an opened mouth in one long breath, as a sigh.

For Erotic-Love: Have a relaxed body with your head tilted slightly back and to the side. Your eyes should be half opened and softly focused. Breathe using shallow rapid breaths in and out of the mouth.

For Tenderness: Have a relaxed body tilted slightly forward. Your head should be slightly tilted left or right. Have a slight smile and relaxed eyes. Breathe using slow even breaths in and out of the nose,

These breathing patterns, body postures, and facial expressions can help trigger the body. Once you are in the proper state you can rehearse your scene. Recognize what happened for your character the moment before, and then jump in. Explore the material and find your truth. Bring it all into being from within you. You are living as this person in this location with these people in this moment. It's all true for you. You won't be acting.

When you do your work this way, people will want to watch what you are doing because they will see a real person experiencing real things. The audience will watch and listen when they sense truth.

Now let's look at how these questions pertain to you in your **real life**:

Who am I? How would you define who you are? Would you like to change who you are in any way? Rehearse that ideal version of you today. Find that new version of you to the extent to which you can, and feel it. Tomorrow do it again. Use each day as another rehearsal day for the new version of you, and over time you will become who you want to be. The daily focus exercises in Chapter Seven will help you create who you want to be.

Where am I? Are you where you want to be? If not, you can imagine yourself in the new location. Rehearse it in your mind. Feel the feelings of being in that new house or that new city. Place the image of where you want to be on a vision board. As you see it and feel it, you will be activating it into your life.

What's my relationship with the people in the scene? Are you with the people you want to be with in your life? If not, you can change by going into new areas with new people who have common interests. Rehearse in your mind meeting those new people. Take actions toward finding new relationships or improving your current relationships.

What do I want? Are you clear on what you want or are you just floating aimlessly? Rehearse going for what you want and be clear on WHY you want it. Imagine yourself signing the mortgage contract and the final payments for your ideal home. Drive by the studios where you plan to work and see yourself entering the gates to go to work on your show. See yourself being a working actor. Whatever it is you want, find a strong enough WHY and the HOW will come to you as you boldly move forward.

What actions will I take to get what I want? Create a list of ten actions for your ideal life, and take one action today toward that vision. Add to your list as you discover new possible actions. Recognize the compound effect of taking consistent action and do something today. Be clear on WHY you are taking those actions and that will help motivate you to follow through.

What is your overall objective? Are you clear on what you want for your life? If you're not, it's not too late. You're still here. You can still be the lead actor in your script. You can still create the life you want if you are willing to focus your energy and move toward your vision. Your future is created today. How do you want to see the world? You can answer the same question as above: My name is _____ and my world is _____.

What do you love about your life? Genuinely embrace all that you love about yourself and your life. There is much to find when you honestly search within. Focus on what you love, and more of that will come to you.

Author Joe Dispenza has some wonderful lessons for creating the life you want, and he backs his teachings with scientific data. I love his message that we will either be defined by "a vision of the future or by memories of the past." What memories of the past are holding you back? What vision of the future do you have for yourself? He also says, "to change your personal reality you need to change your personality." We know how to do this as actors - we are trained to find the characteristics of each character within us. If we want to change ourselves we can commit to developing new character traits for our own lives. We can create who we want to be. To move forward, we must have a vision for our future that is so powerful we won't let anything stop us. As you imagine your future, be sure to feel the feelings of the wish fulfilled.

Steve Martin said, "Be so good, they can't ignore you." To be that good takes daily practice. Steve Martin has been consistently working at a high level because of his dedication to his craft as a writer, comedian and actor. As the saying goes: "those who work a lot work a lot because they work a lot."

Do your preparation work and then play with the scene. Don't try to show all your preparation work, just trust that it is all there. Ask yourself, "what's the first thing I want in this scene?" Determine what that is for your character and then jump in expecting to get it! See what happens. Rehearse and rehearse and discover and discover. As you do your work with a rehearsal-mindset, you will get used to discovering every time, and there will be a new level of magic in your work. The audience won't know what you're going to do or say because you won't know what you're going to do or say until the moment it happens. That's thrilling for you and the viewer!

This level of work comes from discipline and consistency. You can never know when your opportunity will arrive, so you need to always be ready. *Actors aren't hired for their potential, they are hired for what they can do right now.* Success is something we attract by who we become. When you have an approach that will get you thoroughly prepared, no one will be able to shake your confidence. You will be ready.

★ Take any scene and read the entire scene out loud at least twenty times. Get used to being open to letting the scene work on you instead of you working on the scene. Let the scene reveal itself to you. Let the character reveal itself to you. Don't try to control it all with firm choices. Be open.

★ Practice one of your monologues. Don't try to be perfect with it, just experience it moment to moment. Get used to treating it as an exploration rather than a performance, and then use that same rehearsal-mindset each time you work.

★ Do your rehearsals at home in front of a camera set up on a tripod. This will train you to be completely comfortable with being in front of a camera when you work. Let the camera become your friend. When you see a camera on the set you will think to yourself, "There's my friend the camera. I can always be me."

Bob Stivers on *NCIS* (2023)

CHAPTER SEVEN

BE FOCUSED

"The secret of change is to focus all your energy not on fighting the old - but on building the new."

SOCRATES

Just as it is for growth in life, acting is about doing. What are you doing to get what you want? The two most important decisions come down to where you place your focus and what actions you take.

If you want a successful career as an actor, that desire needs to be your focus. When I first moved to Los Angeles to pursue acting, I would think to myself, "what would a successful actor do today?" and then I would act on the thoughts that came to me. The same is true today even after all these years. When I find myself lost as to what to do, I think to myself "what would a successful actor do today?" That's why it is so helpful to have a list of actions printed on a piece of paper and placed on your wall so you can see it every day. As we covered in Chapter One, the list of ten actions will give you clear options to pursue.

Tom Hanks said, "Self consciousness is the death of acting." As actors, we need to be conscious, but not self-conscious. Many actors want to make a good impression, and that mindset puts the actor in his or her head as to "how to do the scene right." In life, people are motivated for a reason. They have a WHY for their actions. In your acting scenes, your focus should be on the why for the character, not the why for the actor. The actor's why is to do a good job to impress the people who may hire them. The why for the character is completely different.

I'll never forget a time when I auditioned for a very popular one-hour drama on CBS. I really wanted to be on the show and was excited to be reading for a great guest starring role. I signed in for the audition and then rehearsed my scenes while I waited in the hallway. My character was the dean of a new college, and the first scene had me happily welcoming the new students. The second scene had me in an interrogation room being accused of murder.

When I arrived in the audition room, I was greeted by ten people all seated in a small office. The cameraman was in the middle. After some pleasantries, the audition started and I was reading with the casting director who was also seated in the middle. As I began the first scene, I noticed the producer right next to the casting director leaned back as though he fell asleep! I couldn't believe what I was seeing. I started speaking the lines my character was saying to welcome the students, and I directed some of those lines toward the sleeping producer. I was trying to wake him up, but he kept his eyes closed. I struggled through the first scene, and the producer opened his eyes when I was done. I then began the interrogation scene and he went back to sleep! I was so flustered by his behavior that I let it bother me through that scene as well. I survived, but I definitely did not do my best work.

The next week in my class, I created an exercise for my students in how to deal with distractions in an audition. I realized I was bothered by the producer's actions because I was letting it affect me personally. My focus was on how his behavior was affecting my desire to get a job. Had I kept my focus on what the *character* wanted and why he wanted it, I could have stayed on track during the audition.

Why is your character saying this? Why is your character doing this? When you focus on the WHY, and you go deep into the WHY, the HOW will take care of itself. Your starting focus should be on the first thing you (as the character) want, and your expectation that you will get it. You then move forward through obstacles, and allow the scene to unfold moment to moment as you pursue what you want.

In my classes, I often use an exercise where I have the actors draw a random acting focus to use as they do their scene. By the time the actors do this exercise, they know their dialogue inside out, and they have covered all the questions from Chapter 6, BE PREPARED. At this point they draw one acting focus for the scene. Some options include: RAISE THE STAKES. LISTEN AND RESPOND. KEEP IT SIMPLE. AFFECT AND BE AFFECTED. BE PRESENT.

When the scene begins, they still put themselves in the circumstance of the scene and they still go for their objective, but their main focus is on the acting focus they drew. At the end of the exercise my only question for them is, "Did you stay on the acting focus for the entire scene?"

What we have discovered through this exercise is it really doesn't seem to matter which focus the actor uses. The result has the actor much more centered and present. There is no pushing, just living. Focusing on the specific focus gives the actor something to do other than trying the do the scene "right." This approach is great to use when you are on set and shooting multiple takes. Use a different one of these focuses for each of your takes and your work will be fully alive and different for each take. You will be engaging to watch because you will be engaged. Your focus puts you in the moment.

I read where Milo Ventimiglia explained how he handled himself in his final audition for the NBC show *This is Us.* The last audition for a series regular role can be a high pressure experience for many actors, but Milo decided to take an easier approach. He said he decided to just BE. That was his focus. Just BE. He

★

In your acting scenes your focus should be on the why for the character not the why for the actor.

⚏

had prepared fully, so he kept his focus simple. Just BE. That audition led to a breakout role that earned him great acclaim and many awards during the long run of the hit show.

Legendary acting teacher Uta Hagen said, "Be active in your scenes and in your life. Good actors look for reasons to do things in a scene, bad actors look for reasons not to." When it comes to our career, we can often become disenchanted with our circumstances and decide to stop taking action for fear of further frustration. There are times when we may find it useful to take a break, but ultimately we must keep on keeping on. That's why your daily habits are so important. If there is something you do every day for your craft and career, it becomes easier to keep moving forward because your acting habits become like brushing your teeth. It's just something you do.

I have been fortunate to play recurring characters on many TV shows, and I attribute much of that experience to how I have handled myself on the job. People want to work with actors who are prepared and happy to be there. When you have a new acting job, I think it's important to not just be ready for how you will do your work as the character, but also how you will handle yourself throughout the studio. You aren't just doing a job, you're building a career. In my class, I have the actors do a daily practice that prepares them to be ready at any time to create a good impression on the set.

What kind of qualities make someone fun to work with? There are many, but here are seven of my ideas. The person is PRESENT, CONFIDENT, HAPPY, OPEN, ACTIVE, LISTENING, and FRIENDLY. I have the actors write these qualities on index cards and randomly draw one of their seven cards to practice each day of the week. The cards will read, "Today's Focus: I will be PRESENT in all my activities." "Today's Focus: I will be CONFIDENT in all my activities." "Today's Focus: I will bring HAPPINESS with me wherever I go." "Today's Focus: I will be OPEN to trying new things." "Today's Focus: I will be ACTIVE today. I will do it now!" "Today's Focus: I will really LISTEN to everyone I meet." "Today's Focus: I will be FRIENDLY today and call people by their first names."

As the actors practice their focus for the day, they begin to notice where they need to grow. They notice, for example, how often they are not PRESENT or not CONFIDENT or not LISTENING. As they choose to be PRESENT or CONFIDENT or to truly LISTEN, they begin to change who they are. They begin to change their personality. Over time, they become the kind of person who is dynamic and fun to be around. When they book a job they naturally behave this way on the set because they act this way every day. By being friendly, calling crew members by their first name, and being a confident person, they create a reputation as someone to hire again and again.

Of all the discoveries we have made in class, the results from our focus work have been the most astonishing ones for me. Your commitment to a specific focus will make you open and present - whichever focus you use. Whether you use a focus in your acting scenes or a focus for your day, you will be grounded and you will grow.

★ Create your list of what you want to focus on for a day. Put each focus choice on a separate index card and randomly draw one for each day. Really commit to the focus for that day. As you practice this regularly, you will notice you are doing more of each of your focuses every day. This practice will help you become who you want to be.

★ When you rehearse your scenes, choose an acting focus such as "RAISE THE STAKES" or "AFFECT AND BE AFFECTED" and completely commit to staying on that focus. Notice how pursuing that focus gets you present in your work.

★ Recognize and accept that what you focus on expands. Choose to focus on what you want more of in your life and in your career.

Lyndon Boyle on *Brooklyn Nine-Nine* (2021)

CHAPTER EIGHT

BE PROFESSIONAL

*"Amateurs sit and wait for inspiration,
the rest of us just get up and go to work"*

STEPHEN KING

People who are successful in any profession recognize they have to raise their standards and develop their skills to the highest level. Whether they feel like working or not, they keep moving forward. One way to keep growing is to find people who will support you as you go through the challenges you face. In my professional class, I set aside some discussion time for the actors to support each other and discuss potential ways for how they can grow as artists and create their own work. I encourage you to find like-minded artists who can support your growth. Spend time with those who have done what you want to do. If you don't have anyone you can meet with now, you can always go online and watch interviews with actors who have achieved a high level of success in their craft and career.

I remember working on the hit show *Brooklyn Nine-Nine* during its final few weeks of production. I was excited to be on the show and was happy that my scenes would be with Andy Samberg and the other main cast. The episode was being shot while the industry was going through the protocols of the Covid pandemic, so the actors were isolated from each other until we got on the set.

I was going to shoot two big scenes on my first day and I figured the first scene would take about two to three hours to shoot, and then the second scene would take about the same amount of time. I was tempted to just review the first scene and then wait to review the second scene later, but something told me to be ready with both. As I prepared in my trailer, I also reminded myself that I fully belonged. Guest actors can sometimes feel like an outsider and let that feeling affect the way they behave on the set, but I was determined to walk on the set as though I was a regular too.

After a shuttle bus took me to the set, the sound operator put a microphone wire on me and then I was guided to a tent with Andy Samberg, Joe Lo Truglio and Terry Crews. I sat down with confidence, and when it was appropriate I chatted with the guys like I was one of them. We all went to the set and the director told the cast that we would shoot *both* scenes back to back. In the past, that kind of surprise may have caused panic for me, but I just trusted that I was ready. We shot the first scene multiple times, and in between takes, I took a moment to get present. In my mind I looked around naming colors, "that couch is tan, that door is brown," etc. Then the director would set up for another take. I would remind myself what my character wanted, and then I would jump in and trust. Over and over, take after take. I was glad I didn't get derailed by the surprise of doing both scenes back to back. I handled it moment to moment. When the week was over and I encountered Andy Samberg in the parking lot, he told me how he appreciated how I handled the episode. He said it was "great to work with a real professional."

What does being a professional actor entail? We must always be ready with our craft when it comes to our work, and we must always be ready with our marketing tools when it comes to our career. We must be pursuing work opportunities and nurturing our industry contacts. We have to keep our eye on the long road because if we don't, the road can come to a sudden stop. I know that from experience.

After I accomplished my goal of being a series regular on a national network show, I took my foot off the gas. I knew I was taking a risk, but quite frankly I didn't care. I had money coming in and I just wanted to be with my family. My parents were going through the final years of their lives and seeing them struggle made me wonder what's the point of life if not to be with those we love and keep our good health for as long as possible.

My focus on acting work dwindled. If I got a call offering me a role, which I did on occasion, I happily took it. I also auditioned for roles, but I'm sure my work did not reflect that of an actor on top of his game. My progress in the business slowed down considerably. Once I looked at my business from a distance, I was able to see where it needed improvement. The craft was not coming from love. The team members (my agents and managers) were not as motivated as before because the lead actor of the team (me) was not inspiring excitement. The decision-makers in casting were not thinking of me because I had fallen off their radar. Time moved on without me. Like a parked car on a side road, I had to find my way back to the highway and make sure I was ready to drive fast once I got there.

The first step toward getting back to work was to make sure my craft was ready at a high level. For me, that meant going back to the basics and finding the love for acting again. The nine-week Foundation Class I took with Howard Fine started to reignite my fire. I remember sitting in the classroom in the middle of the day with many young and beginning actors and it made me wonder why I was there at age 56 - but I knew it was the place for me. I had to either rekindle my love for acting or give it up. Thankfully, I found an approach to the work that helped me to recognize I have a gift to offer that I can truly enjoy exploring and sharing. Once that key ingredient was re-established, it was time to

★

Being a professional actor takes courage and commitment.

♟

focus on the business end. I went about strengthening my team with some new representatives and building new contacts in the industry. An actor's job is similar to that of a farmer: We must always be planting seeds, and harvesting, and building for the future.

To be a professional actor, we must go for it. We can't stick our toe in the water and think we're swimming. We have to jump in fully, just as we do with our scenes. Look at where you are in your career and look at where you are with your craft. Shoot for excellence in both areas. Many actors don't want to focus on the business end, but we have to recognize that when we audition for producers, they are looking at us to see if we can help them make money. They want their show to be successful. Think of it this way - if you were a stock, would people want to invest in you? That's the way agents and managers look at us. When we become great at what we do, people in the industry will want to invest in our future.

When casting directors read actors in their offices or watch actors by self tapes, they usually make snap judgements as to whether or not the actor is ready and if the actor is right for the role. When an actor plays it safe they can easily be forgotten, but when they bring their unique take to the role, they stand out.

As I wrote earlier, I think the two most important choices an actor can make when preparing a scene are to be authentically connected and fully invested.

When you prepare that way, you can trust moment to moment that your work will be engaging, Nevertheless, I do think you can make some other specific choices on how you play the scene based on your explorations in rehearsal. When the writing is good you can trust that the writer has provided what you need - you just need to fully invest. When the writing isn't as good you may need to make efforts to make the scenes more interesting with the choices you make. You can do that by going beat by beat throughout the text and making interesting choices that vary beat to beat. If you choose to take this approach, be sure to justify the WHY for each of those choices so your work will still be authentic.

You can also gain some good ideas from watching the techniques of storytellers. You will notice that good storytellers are engaging to watch because they are telling their truth. They are being vulnerable as they share of themselves. They take you on a journey with them by telling their story in the present tense as if it is happening right now. They occasionally mislead you to keep you guessing what they will say next, and they often take a pause before they share a big reveal. These are all elements you can consider bringing to your scenes.

For example: Have you personalized your character's words and actions so you are telling your truth in the scene? Are you being vulnerable? Is everything happening right here, right now? Now consider: how can you mislead? You can do that by playing against the text. The text gives you the words your character is conveying, so playing against the text can be interesting and surprising to watch. Are there spots in the scene where you can take a pause just as storytellers do before a big reveal? These are all elements that can be fun to explore, and when executed truthfully can make you stand out. The best actors are not afraid to do something different. If it is a legitimate choice that serves the scene, then go for it. Actors tend to think there is a perfect way to play a scene, but that's not true. Austin Butler tells the story of working with Denzel Washington in *The Iceman Cometh* on Broadway. One night, Denzel would laugh in a particular scene, the next performance he may cry at the same point. Which choice was right? Were both choices right? He won a Tony award for his performance. The bottom line is, he was not afraid to take chances. If it was true for him in the moment, it worked. Great actors like Denzel Washington are not afraid.

I think there are three steps to raise the level of your work. Step one is to personalize everything you say and do. Many would-be actors never reach this level. They "act." The second level is to find the roles you are good at and then become great at those types of characters. Completely embody those roles in your own unique and truthful way. The third level is to do whatever you want in your scenes, without concern of judgement. Novice actors are afraid to make a mistake and afraid to be judged. True professionals don't try to prove anything with their work. They fully invest in front of the camera, moment to moment. They follow their impulses. Watch the greats, and that is what you will see.

You can be that way too, but it doesn't just magically happen. Successful actors have tenacity and talent. A sustained career needs *craft*. Just as it is for artists in any craft, the great actors make incremental improvements day by day, month by month, year by year. As the saying goes, "people overestimate what they can do in one year, and underestimate what they can do in ten years."

When I moved to Los Angeles to be an actor, I told everyone I was going to give it ten years. During that time, I fully invested. I was in classes, I did showcases, I made sure I had good photos, and I built strong relationships with my representatives. I made mistakes along the way, but that's the life of an actor.

Once my ten-year period was up, I had to decide whether to continue to pursue acting or to move back to Kansas and try something different. I got quiet and I listened for guidance. Deep inside I sensed I should keep pursuing acting work, and I am so glad that I did. The Del Taco campaign, *My Name is Earl, Raising Hope* and so many more roles came to me after that first decade. All along the way, I prepared for my opportunities because I knew I had to be ready all the time. I have a poem on a plaque in my office entitled "Don't Quit." The last lines read, "Life is strange with its twists and turns as everyone of us sometimes learns... And you can never tell how close you are. It may be near when it seems so far. So stick to the fight when you're hardest hit - It's when things seem worst that you must not quit."

Being a professional actor takes courage and commitment. It's not easy, but there are so many actors who have made it happen and continue to make it happen. If you're willing to stick to the grind, keep exploring and keep growing, you can make it happen too.

★ Take time today for your craft whether you feel like it or not. Eventually, the day will arrive when you will have a "big audition" so practice an audition today. Imagine doing that scene in a casting office and practice how you will be present in the room.

★ Reach out to an industry contact today whether you feel like it or not. It can be through social media or with a written note. Let them know you are still around and on top of your game.

★ Work on your mindset today whether you feel like it or not. Don't spend your time complaining, spend your time committed. Time spent complaining will break you down. Time spent being committed will build you up.

Barney Hughes on *Raising Hope* (2010-2014)

CHAPTER NINE

BE GRATEFUL

"You can't connect the dots looking forward.
You can only connect them looking backward."

STEVE JOBS

As we come to the last chapter of this book, I realize that I have handled my career just as I would an acting scene. I knew what I wanted (to be a successful actor) and I overcame obstacles by taking actions. When my Dad had asked me over thirty years ago how I would make a living in Hollywood I said, "I'm not sure how, but I will." The journey has taken me to many unexpected places and I have met many wonderful people, and I am grateful for it all. It has been an adventure, but it hasn't always been easy.

One of the pivotal moments of my career came when my six-year Del Taco commercial campaign had ended and I had no steady work as an actor. My wife and I were about to have our second child and I was becoming very concerned with how I could support a growing family if

I didn't even know when I would work again. I remember lying in bed and slamming my fist on the pillow as I asked out loud, "What should I do? What should I do!?"

The thought came to me, "I wonder what Sean Whalen is doing?" Sean was an actor who became famous for his performance in a "Got Milk" commercial. Sometimes an actor can become typecast because of commercials, but I figured Sean had overcome that stigma because he had worked quite a bit in films and television. It was odd for me to think of him because I didn't know him well, nevertheless his name came to mind. The very next day I went to Costco and who do you think I saw? Sean Whalen. He was demonstrating a blender. He had been famous, and now he was at Costco demonstrating blenders.

I decided not to talk to him because I definitely did not want *that* job! I went home, and the following day I had a commercial audition. The casting director requested I bring in my passport and so I went home to get it. When I got back to the casting office, who do you think I ran into? Sean Whalen. Sometimes things are meant to be.

He said he was selling blenders part-time and maybe I would like to do it too. He said he had worked 100 days the previous year and made $85,000. What? Really? I thought to myself, if I worked 100 days selling blenders, I could still be available 265 days for acting.

So there I was... a well-known actor, demonstrating blenders at Costco. I was wearing a hair net, standing on my feet for 12 hours a day for ten straight days, and I was definitely not living the dream. The work was difficult and I had to learn new skills in order to sell. The pay was 100% commission and I had to provide all the food I was using to demonstrate the blender, so I was already around $100 in the red as I began each day.

Customers would invariably ask why I was doing that job, but I just told them it was "for fun." I decided I would do my best to make it fun and make some money while staying sharp for my next acting opportunity. The main sales lesson I learned through this experience was that I was much more successful when I focused on the customer than when I focused on my desire to make money. I took the time to learn all I could about the blender, and then I went about focusing on the customer. I made them laugh, I told them about the potential health benefits from using the blender, and I gave them my complete focus. I believed in what I was saying about the blender, so they believed in me. I didn't make a sale every time, but I had way more success and way more fun when my attention was outward rather than inward.

I did not do the blender job at Costco for a complete year, so I don't know if I could've made the amount of money Sean mentioned, but I did end up doing well financially that year. One day while I was at Costco getting ready for another ten-day sales job, I got a call from Greg Garcia. He said he was doing re-shoots for a pilot

★

Your acting skills will help with your life, and your life skills will help with your acting.

♟

and he asked if I would like to play a grocery store manager in a couple of quick scenes. I, of course, said "YES!" and soon I was on the set for what became *Raising Hope*. The show got picked up and before long we were shooting episodes. I did 13 episodes the first season. Before season two began, I was named a series regular. I had come a long way from that moment hitting my pillow only a year before. I think the fact that I was willing to do whatever was necessary to provide for my family may have been the reason this great opportunity came my way. I followed the sign, and I reached my dream. I'm happy to share that Sean also returned to acting and created many films that he has starred in as well.

Back when I was the spokesman for Del Taco, I made a lot of personal appearances and one big event that particularly stood out was when I appeared at the Del Taco location in Hollywood. At that event there were a lot of celebrities and they came up to me wanting a picture with "Dan the Del Taco guy." It was the height of popularity for the campaign. That particular restaurant was at the corner of Santa Monica Boulevard and Highland Avenue. When the campaign was over and I would find myself driving by that location, I would glance over and remember how it was when I was the spokesman for six years. I wondered if I would ever have that kind of success again as an actor. Years went by and then one day I drove by that particular Del Taco location again. I noticed the restaurant had been torn down. Del Taco was all gone, but right on the same piece of land there was a billboard high in the air. The billboard was for a new show on television: *Raising Hope*.

I have had a few signs in my life that indicated I was on the right track, but that's the only time the sign was an actual billboard. I knew then that I was very fortunate. I had worked hard on my craft for many, many years and had invested in my career for many, many years. I was perhaps lucky my opportunity had finally arrived, but I wasn't lucky that I was ready.

As actors, we can't choose how our future will specifically play out, but we can make specific choices each day for how we will grow in our craft and in our career. As we build day by day, week by week, month by month, we set a foundation for success. Once I got back on track with my craft, I regularly started working again in films and television. I have recently been cast to play many dramatic roles I never would have been cast as had I not continued to grow. I'm finding these characters all within me, and this approach has renewed my love for acting.

At the end of every theater performance, the actors go back onstage for a curtain call. It's a wonderful moment where they receive an ovation from an audience that enjoyed their work. It feels good to receive the accolades, but we must remember it is more important to *give* appreciation than to receive.

You succeed in this business because other people want you to succeed. Every step along the way there will be someone who has chosen to work with you, so every step along the way there will be someone you should choose to thank.

I have always been generous with gifts to my agents because I recognize I can't do it without them. They are my team. In December, actors tend to go to agents' offices in large numbers with bottles of wine, gift cards, sweets and other gifts. It can be somewhat overwhelming for agents to receive the same gifts over and over, all at the same time. I think it's more fitting to give gifts at Thanksgiving. The agents receive fewer gifts at that time, and Thanksgiving is literally a time to give thanks.

When I am working regularly on a show, I like to give special gifts to those who have hired me. Greg Garcia created both *My Name is Earl* and *Raising Hope*, so one year I gave him a bobblehead of a character he briefly played on *My Name is Earl*. He loved it. Every year I would give him something unique because he truly changed my life.

The playwright Oscar Wilde said: "The world is a stage, but the play is badly cast." We have the chance to create our own role of a lifetime and choose our own cast. The people you spend your time with will have a great impact on your life, so cast wisely. As I wrote in the introduction, there are two things completely in our control: **our work ethic and our vision for our future**.

Move today toward who you want to be as an actor and who you want to be as a person. Your acting skills will help with your life, and your life skills will help with your acting.

As you finish this book, I want to thank you for giving me the chance to share my perspective on how you can grow into the kind of successful actor and person you are meant to be. Now is your time to shine. Now is your time to create. When an Olympic athlete's time has come to perform, they don't get to ask for more time. They jump in. Your time has come. Jump in!

You'll notice that each chapter of this book started with the word, BE. Who do you want to be in your work and in your life? Your time in this world is short, but you are here now. *This is your time. Be you.* When you are called upon to act in a film or play or television show and the focus is on you, it is *your time*. Find the character within you. It's all within you. Let it out. Let it be.

A CHECKLIST FOR AUDITIONS

When you prepare for an audition don't just phone it in - fill it in. Follow these steps and you will be ready.

Read the scenes out loud 20 times:

★ Let the role work on you.
★ Let the scenes work on you.

Finding the character within you:

★ Who am I?
★ Where am I?
★ What is my relationship with the other people?
★ What do I want?
  (Supply the WHY)
★ What actions will I take to get what I want?
  (Supply the WHY)
★ Where does this character live inside me?
  (How can I use myself?)
★ What do I love about playing this character?

Recording your audition:

★ Block for where the other characters would be off camera.

★ Block for when and how you will use a prop if applicable.

★ Know your lines inside out.

★ Remember the moment before.

★ Prime yourself for the appropriate mental and emotional state.

★ Know the first thing you want.

★ Jump in expecting to get what you want.

★ Allow the scene to unfold moment to moment. Be.

ACKNOWLEDGMENTS

I want to thank my Mom and Dad for encouraging me to follow my dreams. They were fully supportive of my decision to leave Kansas to see what I could become in Hollywood, and they gave me great examples of hard work and generosity.

To my sister Sherry and my brothers Mike and Rick: I have always looked up to you and I appreciate how you have always supported me. I'm glad you're my family. Special thanks to Rex and Judy Thompson for being my California family along with Lance, Kyle and Tad. I have enjoyed all the laughter and inspiration from the Thompson family through the years.

In the film *It's a Wonderful Life,* George Bailey discovered that "No man is a failure who has friends." I am very grateful for all the wonderful people who have become my friends over the years. I have met so many incredible people from all walks of life, and I appreciate your friendship!

Thank you to Glenn Miller, Mickey Taylor and Tim Hackbardt for creating an unforgettable Del Taco campaign. We made some magic.

A big thank you to all the acting coaches who I have studied with over the years, particularly Howard Fine whose influence and words will be found throughout this book.

I appreciate the agents and managers who have represented me, and all the casting directors who have given me the chance to show that I belonged. I am especially grateful to Dava Waite who cast me in multiple shows and introduced me to Greg Garcia. Thank you Greg for changing my life. I'm happy to be one of the Amigos de Garcia.

A big thank you to all the wonderful actors who have taken my "Working Actors Workshop." I love coaching you, and it's been exciting to see you grow into successful actors who are also great people. The best is yet to come.

Finally, I couldn't be more grateful for my family. My son Brett and my daughters Brooke and Brianna have brought me unimaginable joy. I am so proud to be your Dad. I dedicate this book to my beautiful wife Tokiko. You are the most wonderful person I have ever met, and I am so thankful for your endless love and support. You're the best thing that ever happened to me.

RECOMMENDED READING

Fine on Acting: Howard Fine

Seven Spiritual Laws of Success: Deepak Chopra

How to Stop Acting: Harold Guskin

ABOUT THE AUTHOR

Gregg Binkley lives in Los Angeles, California with his wife and three children. He has been a professional actor since 1989 and is also a writer, director, speaker and acting coach. He has been coaching actors at his "Working Actors Workshop" both in person and online since 2017.

For more information:

www.greggbinkley.com
or
www.workingactorsworkshop.net

Made in the USA
Monee, IL
18 February 2024

e8636931-6f21-4406-9644-3da7b1dd7fe0R02